CHICKENS

FARM ANIMAL DISCOVERY LIBRARY

Lynn M. Stone

Rourke Corporation, Inc.
Vero Beach, Florida 32964

PHOTO CREDITS

All photos by the author

ACKNOWLEDGEMENTS

The author thanks the following for assistance in the
preparation of photos for this book: Jerry Johnson/Garfield
Farm Museum, St. Charles, Ill.; Dave Heffernan/Blackberry
Historical Farm Village, Aurora, Ill.

LIBRARY OF CONGRESS
Library of Congress Cataloging-in-Publication Data
Stone, Lynn M.
  Chickens / by Lynn M. Stone.

  p. cm. — (Farm animal discovery library)
  Summary: An introduction to the physical characteristics,
habits, and natural environment of chickens and their
relationship to humans.
  ISBN 0-86593-034-1
  1. Chickens—Juvenile literature. [1. Chickens.] I. Title.
II. Series: Stone, Lynn M. Farm animal discovery library.
SF487.5.S76 1990
636.5—dc20   89-29872
                    CIP
                    AC

TABLE OF CONTENTS

CHICKENS

People admire birds because they can fly. Yet the most common bird in the world—the chicken *(Cellus domesticus)*—would not make a good flying instructor. At best, chickens can fly a few hundred feet.

Like their wild relatives, chickens have short, rounded wings. With their fairly long legs and toes, chickens run better than they fly. But flier or not, the tasty chicken is probably the most important bird on earth.

Today, chickens are sometimes known as domestic **fowl.**

HOW CHICKENS LOOK

Chickens are plump birds with short, sharp beaks and blood-red **combs** and **wattles.** The fleshy comb rises like a crest along the chicken's head. The wattles droop below the chicken's chin.

Chickens come in a wide range of colors. Combs, wattles, and the length of feathers vary widely. The Japanese Yokohama chicken may have tail feathers 18 feet long.

Bantam chickens may weigh as little as one pound. The biggest chickens top 12 pounds.

WHERE CHICKENS LIVE

Would you like to count the world's chickens? Don't volunteer for the job! There are some nine billion chickens on earth. Perhaps three billion of them live in the United States.

Until the early 1500's, North America had no chickens. Spanish explorers brought the first chickens to North America.

Today, China, Russia, and the United States are the greatest chicken producing countries. Almost all countries raise some chickens, and chicken eggs and meat can be found throughout the world.

Wild turkey

BREEDS OF CHICKENS

Early chicken farmers found that their chickens were not exactly alike. Some were bigger than others. Some had longer feathers.

The farmers began to keep chickens with similar looks together. The big chickens produced more big chickens. The long-feathered chickens had more of the same.

These new groups, each somewhat different from the others, became known as **breeds.**

There are now over 200 breeds of chickens. Only a few are important to chicken farmers. Many breeds are raised just because people enjoy their curious behavior or color.

Barred rock chicken hen

Rooster wakes the farm

Hen incubating eggs

WILD CHICKENS

The closest relatives of domestic chickens are four kinds of wild jungle fowl found in Asia. The red jungle fowl was probably the bird first used as barnyard chickens over 4,000 years ago.

Turkeys are related to chickens. But the chicken's closest cousins, next to jungle fowl, are quail, partridge, and pheasants.

Like chickens, these birds have short, sharp bills and feet that are made for scratching on the ground and running.

Ring-necked pheasant

BABY CHICKENS

Baby chickens develop in an egg for about three weeks. The egg is warmed by the mother chicken or in an **incubator.** An incubator warms with electric heat.

Newly-hatched chicks are covered by soft, fuzzy feathers called down. They can walk and feed themselves soon after hatching.

By five months of age, a female chicken, or **hen,** can begin laying eggs.

Chickens raised mainly for their meat reach market size in just eight or nine weeks.

HOW CHICKENS ARE RAISED

Many farmers throughout North America have a few chickens. The chickens live in a barn or shed. They may lay their eggs wherever they find loose straw or in a nesting box.

The largest number of chickens in North America are raised on farms which produce only chickens. One farm may house over one million chickens.

Many chickens never leave the large buildings where they are born until they are taken to market. Machines supply their food and water and clean their cages.

Chicken house

HOW CHICKENS ACT

Days begin early for flocks of barnyard chickens. The **rooster** crows its first loud cock-a-doodle-do before the sun rises!

Roaming flocks of chickens spend much of their time scratching the soil for seeds and insects. Hens with eggs sit on their nests.

Chicken flocks have leaders and followers. Strong chickens tend to bully the weak ones. Chickens can bloody each other with their beaks and **spurs.**

Roosters can be quite fearless. They may even try to drive people away from their hens.

Rooster

HOW CHICKENS ARE USED

Every American, on the average, eats about 45 pounds of chicken meat and 300 chicken eggs each year.

Chicken flesh is low in fat. As more people try to reduce the fat in their diet, chicken meat will grow in popularity.

Scientists use chickens to produce certain medicines. Fly fishermen use lures made from chicken feathers.

People raise fancy chickens as a hobby or for show.

Some breeds have been developed just for fighting. Chicken fights are not legal in the United States.

Glossary

breed (BREED)—closely related group of animals that came about through man's help; a type of domestic chicken

comb (KOME)—a red, blood-filled crest along a chicken's head

fowl (FOWL)—any bird, but especially domestic ducks, geese, chickens, and turkeys

hen (HEN)—a female chicken or any of several other female birds

incubator (INK u baiter)—device in which eggs and/or chicks are kept warm

rooster (ROO stir)—an adult male chicken

spur (SPUR)—a stiff, sharp toe on the back of a chicken's legs

wattles (WATT ulls)—red, blood-filled flesh that droops below a chicken's chin

INDEX